Mother Animals and Baby Animals

SCOTT, FORESMAN AND COMPANY • GLENVIEW, ILLINOIS
Dallas, Tex. • Oakland, N.J. • Palo Alto, Cal. • Tucker, Ga. • Brighton, England

ISBN 0-673-10603-9

mother animals

baby animals

mother animals

baby animals

mother animals

baby animals

mother animals

baby animals

mother animals

baby animals

mother animals

baby animals

mother animals

baby animals

Name the animals.